Allowed and Aloud
selected poems by gus Simonovic

Edited by Laurice Gilbert

www.PRINTABLEREALITY.com
... poetry Co-lab. live literature . spoken word .

Its all about you and me now. Just you and me.
And a little bit about it and her and him and them.
Finally alone. Finally together. Finally at ease ...
on paper and on audio.
Open or play the book, open up and lets read each other.
I have no better way to get to know you, but to share.
Is not as if I wrote all the lines in this book,
even that my name is printed on the cover.
And, if you don't feel that some of those lines are "yours",
you have discovered another you.

Enjoy the experience of the attempt to be an inaccurate interpreter of my own experience. I can only hope that this attempt in using word management, to go beyond meaning of words, will mean something to You ... and her and him and us.

This book is dedicated to You!

© 2014, Printable Reality/gus Simonovic
ISBN 978-0-473-27366-8

"Stage2Page" publishing series #1

stage2 page

By purchasing this book you get a free audio and e-book download, please email gus@printablereality.com for the access code.

ALL RIGHTS RESERVED. This book contains material protected under International and NZ Copyright Laws and Treaties. Any unauthorized reprint or use of this material is prohibited. No part of this book may be reproduced or transmitted in any form or by any means, electronic or mechanical, including photocopying, recording, or by any information storage and retrieval system without express written permission from the author / publisher.

Whats Inside?

Editors Note 6

Part I: Poems about You

your heart 7
Another Messenger 7
Sunrise on the West Side 8
Attend 9
Love is 9
Birth of the Nation 10
Yeast 11
Comma Ellipsis 11
Cosmos of Hearts 12
Crown of Thorns 13
Stone Precious 13
Don't Ask the Fish 14
Numb 14
Ensnare 15
Thief 15
Everything ... and a Purple Lipstick Dress 16
One Day 17
From Somewhere to Knowhere 18
H to gO2 19
Holy Daze (Waterfall) 20
In Between Dreams 21
In Eight Scenes 22
Isotopes 23
Island and the Sea 24
Justice 25
One Zero, One Page 27
Read as you write/ Write as you dream 29
Stereotype 30
The Look of Love 31
Pen Friend 32
Where Shadows Meet 33
The Door 34

Part II: Poems about Me

44	35
Message	36
Available For Parties	37
Equator	38
Figurative Sense	39
Fire ... Place	39
Here	40
Fisherman	41
Mirror Mirror	42
Insomnia in a Daydream	43
Tense Free	44
Lifetime Warranty	45
Slam	46
Kidnapped	47
Monday, the day after Sinday	48
Man = Heart (From 5 to 5 till 5 past 5)	49
Out of Step Parade	51
six days and one Wednesday	53
Spinning the Real	56
Striptease	57
Time Speaks	58
Summer Love	59
Superhero	60
The Golden Boat	61
The Heart Asks for Pleasure First	62
The Nine Circles of Heaven	63
Visionary Indecisiveness	64
The Place where Something-Outside-of-You is Thinking	65
Pure Noise	66
There, Maybe	67

Part III: Poems about Us

Sixty Nine	69

Editors Note:

When Gus asked me to edit his collection, I was delighted to accept the invitation. I confess that my eagerness was more about me than him - I love to edit. Nevertheless, I wouldn't have done it if I didn't enjoy his work, which I'd previously had the pleasure of both reading and seeing performed.

The poetry entrepreneur, which is how I categorise Gus, is a rare beast. This one's list of accomplishments is staggering, given that he came to New Zealand from Serbia with a rather urgent need to come to grips with English. He has claimed that his English vocabulary is still limited, but that he enjoys words he hasn't heard or used before. This was evident in the poems I read for this collection, several of which sent me to my dictionary. I like that in a poet.

I also like that he uses the language joyously, playing with repetition in a semi-hypnotic way to reinforce his enthusiasm.

As an immigrant, Gus brings an observer's eye to life in New Zealand, and his poetic voice is distinctive in its slightly off-key English. Added to his unique grasp of metaphor, his voice is a pleasure to read and deserves to be disseminated widely. My favourite line, heard first in an innovative performance, and greeting me like an old friend when it appeared in the collection, sums it all up for me:

> *"I think without an accent
> but that's not how I talk."*

Bringing a collection of his poems to the poetry-reading public is a generous and valuable gesture by Gus, and I hope readers enjoy them as much as I did throughout the editing process.

Laurice Gilbert, April 2014

Laurice Gilbert is President of, and magazine editor for, the New Zealand Poetry Society, with poems published in many New Zealand and international journals and anthologies, both in print and online. She is the current Featured Poet International at Muse-Pie Press (USA), and published her first collection, My Family & Other Strangers, in December 2012. She is currently working on a joint collection with Portuguese poet Hugo Kauri Justo.

Part I: Poems about You

your heart
blank
like a piece of paper
my heart
drunk
full of love-ink

distance
heavy
like a paperweight

singing
the song
from whistle to growl
a song
no ear
would like to hear

Another Messenger

I bring you: one cubic metre of thoughts
and a gram of love.

OK, bring them to the kitchen please
I am cooking.

I don't think that love will fit through
your door.

That's what happens when you think
too much.

Sunrise on the West Side

The day was grey;
almost as if night was lit –
sunrise on the west side.

We went for a walk.
She felt like sand,
I felt like grass.

If it was a dream
I would say that I saw a bench,
a bench that wasn't there before, or after
not that we ever sat down for a rest.

If it was a dream
I would say there was a monument,
a monument to nothing.
Not that we ever wanted it to be there, or to something.

If it was a dream
I would say there was a dog,
who scared our expansive hearts, and fear
harmonised our discordant minds;
there was a big white box,
on wheels.
Which disappeared to give way to her story.

If it was a dream
I would say that I saw another colour.
The colour orange, colour of my T-shirt,

colour of the east skies.
Colour of the flower
that she gave me;
orange flower, that she found,
thinking that it was me.

Attend

in a moment
she whispered

in a moment …
and time bent

in a moment
she said

in a moment …
and light took a curve

in a moment
I asked

in a moment?
and gravity lost its pull

at that moment, I knew
I love you

because
I still believe you

Love is
like playing tennis without scoring
Without lines and double faults
And enjoying it

Love all

Birth of the Nation

It was a long-drawn-out affair.
Wait fell in love with Delay,
everything went light and slow.
Wait's non-reactive nature got on very well with
Delay's phlegmatic disposition.

They didn't want to rush into anything.

So the wedding was postponed many times
until the day.
The whole universe was present
galaxies of deferral,
family and friends travelling many light years
without arriving.
The cake was not cut and bells rang ad infinitum,
a pause-dance was played and a hold-up hymn was sung.
Speeches were interluded
while every present given, kept taking
time.

After a longish wait, Wait conceived,
the big future - Delay was on its prolonged way.
But it had no name.
Hindrance was chosen for a godfather
and decided to postpone any decisions.

After nine light months
Hibernation was born.

Yeast

Oh my God.
If I look like a frog, I feel like one;
I want to jump out of my skin.
What use is skin if you are not touching it?

Oh my God.
If I look like a dragon, I don't feel like one;
just a frog that blew on the fire to keep warm.

I gave you binoculars. I gave you a compass.
I gave you a watch. Every morning every night
I grow and put on fragrance so you can see me,
so you can smell me; during the day I shrink so I won't
scare you when you find me.

Reluctantly I sprinkle the yeast of longing on the dough of
time.Dreaming of your hands breaking the bread,
and finding the hidden coin of love.

Comma Ellipsis

no quotation marks its hard to make sense ellipsis
its hard to make sense question mark
sense was never made semicolon
it's hyphen hard hyphen to hyphen make hyphen sense
it's hard to make sense exclamation point because colon
yes it is hard to make sense comma
comma comma comma comma comma comma comma
comma ellipsis
the hardest thing is to make sense full stop

dash its hard to make sense even in parentheses
dash

Cosmos of Hearts

hide your lips
don't say words, that they
want to say
hush them up
even if nobody is listening
save your ears

cover the mirror
kiss the moon instead
moon … moon … moon
the moon is full of crescents
on all sides
popping up like kisses in the sky
smiling, capping, turning, tide-ing its sharp ends

it whispers soft light to guide our hearts
as every heart is a planet,
round, ticking, listening in
revolving around the moon
heart stays always full
on all sides
it pumps out words to occupy our lips
it pumps out thoughts to occupy our steps
as our beings revolve around our beloveds' hearts
moving, feeling, screaming, writing, filling verses of our
silent universes

shhh …keep quiet
let the moon do the talking
words wonder, in and out of the shadow
thoughts wander in and out of shape
but they are no things,

nothings
if we don't talk about them

Crown of Thorns

Your pain, a shadow of my wound.
Your happiness, the measure of my prayers.

If you are on the North Pole, tell me;
I will come and freeze next to you.

But if you are making a box for me
and digging a hole,
you will have to come
and cremate me with your kiss.

This love will not fit in any coffin.

Stone Precious

I was skimming over tears.
But couldn't get to the other side.

I was talking to words. I was talking to words
and I couldn't make my point

I didn't audition for this act, I didn't apply for this role,
I was cast in stone.

I remember how the silence sounded before.
Now, silence resonates – granite.

When I am brave enough to look around
I trap an image in the mirror
and eyes confirm a pact of silence.

I was going to run and stop you at the door.
But I couldn't stop myself, watching you.

Don't Ask the Fish

Don't ask a fish how big the fishbowl is

Don't ask the water how many fish there are

Don't ask the water what happened yesterday

Don't ask a fish what colour the water is

Don't ask the bowl why it is not singing

Don't ask a fish about your dream

Don't ask the water why the bubbles

Don't ask the bowl about the fish or water

Don't ask

Numb

Fell numb before I had a chance to ask
woke up just before I grasped an answer

Bible next to my pillow
comic book in my hands

I found someone who's got skin like yours
so - life is good!

       on the surface

Ensnare

I loved him
but he was too busy loving me
to notice.
I planned for our future
but he was too busy analysing the past,
to follow.

I wanted to adopt
he was having too much fun playing with his toys
to commit.

I kept depositing into our joint account
but he was too busy spending
to take interest.

I hated him.
He was trying too hard to get over me
to care.
I called, for permission to love someone else
but he was too busy
to talk.

Thief

In a dream
I put pen to paper.
I extract you
from lines and commas
I steal you from my own poems.
The poems
shrink to syntax
as life becomes
a living dream.

I love you like I love my poems.

Everything ... and a Purple Lipstick Dress

I want you to go up there and be, be that tree, take
off your shoes and dance off your roots, loosen your
hat, lose your head, sprout, burst, flourish

I want you to fly up there, with your wings, and be
be that bird, your days to fly and your nights to rest
your songs to sing, your own chicks - to nest

I want you to roll out there and become a dice
all square and cubic, all round and dotted, and
let people play with you, let numbers define you

I want you to step out, out there and be a street sign
tall and lonely, at the side of the road, deaf and mute
a warning, a pointer, an advisor and a saviour

I want you to pace in there and come to be a chapel
a prayer place without a preacher, deity or a symbol
a chapel of ease, the holy place I can be devoted to

I want you to buy a lipstick, red? no! purple
put it all over my lips, and let me entwine, make me
lace kisses on your skin, into an ultimate purple dress

I want you to drift, into the sea, like a stone washed away
by a big wave, taken to the depths, meet starfish, sharks
and shells, splash, crash, and return like sand, with a tide

I want to draw you as a cartoon character, with no limits,
morph, so that you can stay perfect
as you are, in your purple lipstick dress

One Day

This morning my tongue was numb
I wasn't sure if it was there, in my mouth.
Oh, I will not be able to speak anymore.

Run to the mirror in search of my tongue
only to discover my ears have grown huge
and my eyes are on long sticks.
At least I will hear and see well.

Some alien insect only I had no legs, just feet.
Even though walking was a funny exercise,
I felt very good, and   wanted
to walk out and face the world.

No one noticed me anyway –
as if I always looked like this,
as if everybody had huge ears, and eyes on sticks.

As I walked, legs grew out and met my feet,
gave me extra stability, more ease, more confidence.

I was a part of the world.
My mind was my friend.
I couldn't talk
        everybody was my friend
I could see and hear
        there was no reason for opinion.
I could go anywhere.
My seven-mile steps, my 360 degrees vision.
I could hear the moon moving.

That's how I came to the zoo.
To put myself on display,
to cage this stage.
To be something I always wanted
- even for a day –
one of you.

From Somewhere to Knowhere

A movement:
Believers calmly cross the river on the ferry.
Birds on the power-line fly to the monastery.

A quest:
A quest for the treasure of truth
using a map of habits.

Losing the seasons of life
investing in a gratifying grave,
like seeking magic in boredom.

When life breaks
Memories fall out of the cracks.

From somewhere to knowhere …

Genesis,
Belief is foundation
Movement is creation,
Stopping is confirmation.

Belief is begotten from doubt!
And it will disappear in doubt
Surrounded by doubt
If there were no doubt, there could be no belief.
The base of all things is …
Belief.

Truth?

Believe,
we will find the truth
once the last believer is dead.

H to gO2

A drop of water, huge as an ocean,
unnecessary as an umbilical cord.
You, as far away as India,
as close as a Siamese twin.

In one drop, as many tears,
as there are joys.

Only one drop. How can we swim?
If we move too fast continents will divide,
planets will vanish. If we stay still we will drown.

And we float
in an imaginary boat in an imaginary direction.
And we float, adjusting the sails
waiting for a favourable wind.

One drop. And we are so wet!
Sometimes splashed. Sometimes sprinkled.
Sometimes rained on. Sometimes washed.
Sometimes drenched. Sometimes dry.

On that one drop – two poles: plus and minus,
masculine and feminine, north and south.
And currents, whirlpools, icebergs, monsoons.
We don't need air ... earth ... fire.

Like a two-cell organism in a solution of love
one drop!
Like a medium of osmosis
necessary for symbiosis.

I don't mind if it's a bit cold,
so long as it doesn't evaporate.

Holy Daze (Waterfall)

That Winter, in the middle of the Spring
hopping from boulder to boulder,
the missed person. You arrive.
   on the moon. Tranquil.
and the way you don't move
shapes my tides.

The silence is deep
   soundtrack for romance.
I, all over the moon
you, all over the earth.
     what we like, we don't like to rush
we let it fall.

Then you move
climb down to the clouds
turn mystery into the mist
drop
to the sea
knowing my arms will be there
to wave to you
catch you
into the wave
to be a wave
next to me
friable freefalling.

This Summer, in the middle of the Fall
I am inundated
I am water
I am not in love
love is not what it was.

It's a long fall.

In Between Dreams

Twilight suburb of nebula
stars out of constellations
every cloud has a quick-silver lining,
Night-air is mercury knitted.
Plagiary autumn of the lonely,
hermit city in a deep sleep
snoring, roaring
lost in its own mind.

Highway of dreams
moon pointing the way.
Knocks on my window
moonlight –
reflection of delight
night-time colour to my day-dreaming.
In the city that is out of its mind, at the time never lost
on track to the well-unknown,
to the foretold destination.

At that time, we're in the same world –
The World In Between Dreams.

Sometimes time is the Time
Sometimes time is only a time
At the time when time is everything
we are nothing but timers.
Now, at this time, I sense we have another, more
significant, Now
      to come.

Give dream a chance, give dream a chance ...

In Eight Scenes

Scene one:
She approaches him, with poise. It seems that she is looking him in the eye. The audience is engaged, quiet, almost interested. He is interested, quiet, almost engaged.

Scene seven: memories ...
When they first met, she had that spark in her eye. She was hiding in the darkness, behind that spark. Casting a shadow over his role, she played her part.

Scene twelve:
"Here is my map, a Map you will never need". After acting out hesitancy, he accepts it with great import. And the curtain billows as a violent storm shakes the stage.

Scene twenty-two: off stage ...
The arena is swept by the wind. The set looks ghostlike, blue, white and gusted. Pure? Or forsaken? They walk out on to that land, the land of the long white cloud.

Scene twenty-seven:
On stage again, same parts, different plays. Same make-up, new viewers. "Give up. Why, why don't you just give up!" she cries. As if that is a choice anyone can make.

Scene thirty: his plea ...
"Take me off the cloud, put me where you keep pyjamas. Take me, put me in your toothbrush holder. Take me somewhere we can sit in the dark, watch other players."

Scene forty-three:
She is still waiting for his answer. "I'll give up," he replies, more to the listeners. "One day, I will". How many curtains before the applause, how many lives before the bow?

Scene fifty-eight: the morning ...
Bell rings, or the alarm clock. Curtain goes up, or to the side. Light looks at her, he looks at the light. The audience never sleeps. Someone delivers the coffee and fresh roles.

Isotopes

once upon a rhyme
for an immeasurable quantum of time
two beams of light bumped into each other
connecting light years to the very source of light
bending the line of immanence and transcendence
bouncing off drops
forming the rainbow

they met and they stayed still
in-line, in-light, in colour
following still uncreated laws of physics
or any other form of stillness
or rule, or rhyme

day by night, second by heart beat
word by silence, line by bow
molecule by atom ... connection is breaking
but not the need for connection

and when the last atom breaks
we are found in all that empty space
much vaster than any sidereal distances
space between forgotten and lost particles and particulars
inner-space, that is somewhere out there
heels over head

breaking
creates a single drop
on my cheek

that forms a rainbow
in my eye
a rainbow so tick ... solid,
like a bridge I can cross
to finally meet you

when I say meet you
I mean meet you ... again
as we already met before

two lines of rhyme
from another poem
two beams of light
in a single teardrop

Island and the Sea

look from the cloud, how waves weave
an infinite white ring, enclosing the island

you can see their connection, hot and cold
day and night, year on year, in and out

yesterday we held hands on that beach
today you ask me to be your friend

last week we splashed in a labour of love
now, you expect me to labour your point

my words will promise anything, as I am rational man
my heart will continue to sing, as I am poet

you can turn my words into rocks and sand
to protect yourself from the song of the waves

for what can the sea and the island be –
other than lovers or friends?

Justice

They put on the fireworks and dress us up in red,
they wear a beard and put antlers on us.
They drive snowmobiles
and they say "celebrate! it's a New Year."
The new year that will bring us new debt
but the calendar is not working anymore,
seasons are changing quicker,
debt is on the loose and the clock
has lost its cuckoo.

The stop-watch is reduced to a stop.
Judging by Wall St time, they think we are moving

Frivolous farmer I am, visited by the fairy.
I plough on my dream-land,
water a swamp of utopian ideas –
shaking the trees in this fruitless orchard.

Look at the other farmers, the corporate hands that feed them.
Docile growers, noble shepherds,
benevolent gravediggers.
Corn is their flower,
grains are their brains,
rice is their high, livestock their poetry,
watches are their compass,
wallowing in the ecstasy of prescribed success and progress.

The chance to prune is a chance to grow.
Chance to cut is a chance to cure.
Chance to harvest is a chance to seed.
Chance to live is a chance to fight.

And I dance   dance
like a perennial catkin,
following the red star,
on the road named recycled time
          I hear Heaven's soundtrack.

In the land of peace and profits
the fields are woven by prayers.
In the air full of hope
          a surfeit of blame.
Visceral feeling of obituary gravity
          life ebbing away in the way that leads us
to the estuary of Heaven.

The sundial is drifting.
Hoard up our time!
to replay
          spend the present to buy the future.

The relentless way from Hope-town to Heaven
stops at our imaginary meeting point:
Lack of light, dyeing colours, white swallows
Coming from the north. Abandoned paddocks
Dying landscape. Still life.

Eyes closed. Rain on my face.
As if it matters. As if it mattered. As if it will matter –
everything reminds me of you, anyway.

Renegade farmer goes back to ploughing.
Jester lost in tragedy,
trying to trade tears for breath.
To breathe only to sigh
          to live only to waft, waiting for the left way.

The real new year is still to come.

One Zero, One Page

this is a poem
about one zero

this is a poem
about 1.7 trillion lines
one line
for every dollar
classified
spent
every year
every year ... every year
on

what? 1.7 trillion dollars a year?
hold on –
let me put those zeroooooooooos in place
No that might ruin the flow of this stanza

WARNING:
next stanza contains too many zeros

1.7 000
000 000
000 000
how do we get rid of one?

it's not about how much they spend to make the product
but how the product is spent

how many happy customers benefit
from this great number of zeros

how much National Security is improved
and national interest expended

how many jobs get created
and everything else dominated

by those zeros
zeros zeros zeros …
zeros that breed zeros

how free can my verse be?
to free up one zero off that number
and return numbers to numbers, words to words;
to stop the war between logic and maths,
to let us out of this anti-society

how light can my verse be?
to rid us of riding with that one heavy zero
to make us walk upright again

shall we stop using O's, because they look like zeros?
how many trillions-of-what do we need to spend
to fight rockets, bombs and bullets
how many calculations and equations
just to eliminate one zero
just one zero

how many peace actions, art projects, how many occupies,
how many selections and elections,
how many revolutions and evolutions,
how many Gandhis and Lennons,
how many mushrooms and Ground Zeros
how many cries, how many lives
how many Writings on The Wall

to delete that One Zero from the end of That Number
and make this poem fit
on one page

Read as you write/ Write as you dream

Tonight,
I listen in to the wind and the leaves
to shivers, raindrops and megabytes,
to breathing and little colours
to silence, thoughts and scents.

I am waiting with eyes closed, senses open.

I stand on the shore of my dreams,
telling myself a bedtime story.

So excited I am scared I will forget
to breathe when I fall asleep.
I am listening in to reach you.

I hear movements.
Clouds decorating the sky.
Saturn's rings circling.
A spider as it weaves its web.
Mushrooms as they grow in the forest.
Oyster-shells as they form pearls.
I hear birds returning from the south.

When morning comes I have no words.
I am waiting to hear you,
to feel your touch so I can talk.

The moon is close, behind the clouds.
The sun is rising out of the sea
and you are everywhere in between.

Postcard from Wherever-you-want City
on the shore of my dreams.

Stereotype

On your forehead, intelligence
In your hair, a breeze
On your cheeks, freckles
In your eyes, a twinkle
On your chin, a dimple
On your lips, a rosebud
In your mouth, pearls

In your heart, passion and hope
In your chest, courage and belief
In your soul, honesty and love

Your neck, an apple
Your breasts, all other fruit
Your belly, an endless plain
Your bottom, a hillock
Your legs, a rhythm
Between your legs, fire and water

And in your head?
A Stereotype.

The Look of Love

She was French, or Swiss maybe.
She was a traveler,
a gift from
a friend of a friend.
Brakes on her car didn't work;
we almost crashed into somebody
in the liquor-shop car park.
She had a girlfriend
back home,
she told me.
She stole a bowl of ketchup (like, a big bowl)
from the restaurant.

The bathroom light in the hotel
didn't work.
We got an upgrade and a late check out.

Now, at midday,
I'm sitting on the sunny balcony
on the top floor
of the highest building in town,
starving.
Bright sunshine bounces off
wrinkled white sheets,
and washes the lines off her face.
She semi-opens her eyes,
looks at me.
Her look
looks
as if she loves me
or loved, somebody else.
While I was eating last-night's pommes frites
coloured in red.

Pen Friend

one Tuesday at the writers' class
I met Mr Digby and his creative lines

the lines on his face, a book almost finished
lines in his poems, jewels that could never perish

I asked for more and he didn't use a computer
so we posted metrical lines to each other
I strained and stretched, computed, printed
and enveloped my humble song offerings

and waited, waited for his heart-wit replies
while his trembling hand wrote verse without effort

lines came alive: bold, italic and over-scored, so youthful
feeding me, grafting me, lining my poetic pockets

until last Tuesday, when my poem was returned
with the prosaic "no-longer-at-this-address" line
I ran to grab the big book, found the right White page,
printed and re-sent the enveloped poem to new address

trying to remember if he mentioned his move
and a letter came back, like the good old days

with a short unsigned note, as if from heaven:
send no more bills, Mr Digby has died.

This Tuesday, one more line around my eyes
privileged to be next in line to inherit some of his lines
I will stop sending letters, but not printing poems
until one of those Tuesdays when I can hand-deliver them

to Mr Digby the poet.

Where Shadows Meet

the sun is young, the shadows long, culpable
as if carrying remainings of the night
from the other side of the sphere

moon still pasteled in the sky
its invisible body effortlessly wearing its visible part as a
hat, as it conducts another morning-symphony of
invading waves

a scattering of copper-colored clouds,
floating on the surface of the sky,
mirroring a few early sails on the harbour

trees tremble and flicker like football players
offering to exchange shirts after a match

one more time

early risers, denizens and citizens
walking their best, elongated friends.
workers, disappearing into buses,
reducing their individual body contours
into a closely dispersed row of head-shapes,
striding across the curbs and bus stations

a bunch of hysterical 1000-kilos-of-steel cleverly+designed
to carry one or two bodies
noisying around, chasing their silhouettes

city buildings, somehow bigger,
desiccated. as if crossing the highway
angling to bath in their park-grounds-skyline

Rangitoto throws its shadow across the Harbour
to wake up Auckland one more time
the bridge arches like a party balloon
carries the weight of the city, as it hugs its profile
in the water

ocean waves twirl by the beach,
where Chinese are dancing their tai-chi tango of shadows -
backward and forward,
pirouetting by the port on their blue and white tiptoes
(not to scare the dinosaur cranes)
as they sneak in under the bridge
to embrace the city
and take all our shadows away

one more time

The Door

Closed door in the middle of the open space –
a pheasant sitting on the invisible fence.

Certainty of surprise –
sensation of the physical absence of something.

Thoughts illicit, heart chained
Spirit grounded, logical negativism
The weakness of now, the power of then
Telepathic omission

The time of non-miracles will soon be over.
I am collecting feathers

not to fly.
Only to look beautiful
for when the door is open.

Part II: Poems about Me

44

I load my intention for connection
onto the ferryboat.
They've seen it – it's huge!
So they make me buy a family pass.

You sit looking into the wake
face to the waves, back to the all,
expression hidden by the wind
listening to the sounds of before.

It's not that you don't like me
it's not like you're being remote
it's just that I don't know you
it's just, you don't know me.

I - on the bow, you - on the stern. The distance is vast.

To reveal intention I need attention.
Jump off the ferry?
Would be like a leap into my past.
Wait for the landing?
Would be a missed chance.
So? I pause.

I p a u s e.

And … you turn.
44 seconds before we first talk
44 minutes before our first lunch
44 weeks before our first baby
44 years before … I jump off the ferry.

Message

An egg was glued to my windscreen.
At first I didn't see it clearly and I turned the wipers on
Only then I didn't see anything, blinded by the yolk.

There was something epicene about that egg.
There is something incipient about every egg,
We have all started off as an egg,
There is a hatch and a catch in each egg.
An Egg ...
like an eleventh commandment,
like the second purpose of love.

... man is devoid of common sense
and I am that man this morning.

Maybe something was written on the shell,
or there is some symbolism in the white?
Maybe you just wanted me to wash the vehicle,
or to show me how it is to drive from the passengers seat?

An egg out of its nest,
An egg to put me to the test.
Was it from you? Was it an egg?
Am I becoming egg-o centric?

and did I get the message?

Available For Parties

I was once invited to be a brick in the wall.
What kind of party is that?
Maybe because I was previously known
as a stitch in the curtain.
 But curtains hang,
 and what was going to hold up this wall
 if all the bricks were as airy as me?

I was once invited to be a light in a tunnel
And they wanted me to RSVP.
I asked how many lights are going to be there
They said: this is not a party. This is a performance.

I was once invited to be a part of a bouquet.
They said: "It's going to be beautiful".
  "Under one condition", I replied:
  "I am not going to be a flower".
 What else? they asked. The cellophane, if I may.

I was once invited to be a number
In a padlock combination
   Only I had to decide which One.

Not long ago I was invited to be a wave in the ocean
and I practised, practised.
   By the time I got there, it was low tide.

Once I was invited to be a member of the party.
It was going to be a small party made up only
of people who had never won Lotto
   I couldn't imagine being with losers.

Once I was invited to be a word in the poem
And I decided to be:
The last line.

Equator

If words are the stars,
poems are constellations.
You need to know the figure
to shape out meanings.
And wherever you move
every nightsky speaks
a different language.

I crossed the line -
and left my northern stars
at that invisible border.
They were confiscated
by the equatorial customs office.
But I smuggled my poems with me
so I can still speak to you.

I exchanged my Little Dipper
for Magellanic clouds.
Instead of Polaris
Sigma Octanis brightens my horizon.

And I reach up high and I dig down deep
like every plant that has been
pulled out by its roots.
Lucky to have Leo and Orion
to help me bear my Southern Cross.

Figurative Sense

This is where I come, as a centipede. With one hundred legs, only a hundred steps away from home. My emotional backyard.

Here it is. A place with holes, a Holy place where unexpressed feelings are buried. A minefield of a hundred mines. A poem.

A hundred mines for a hundred lost loves; hundred legs, for every future one. A hundred steps, for a centipede. One for a man.

Back home, I turn up the volume on my clock and sit. Sit there with my clock. Listening to time pass, second by second.

Like a time mine. Like steps. It seems as if I am waiting, yet I am just about to leave, any second. In one step. Like every time.

Fire ... Place

I can write to you without the ink
I can read to you with my eyes closed
I can call you without a sound
I can sleep with you with my eyes open
I can dance for you without movement
I can grow on this tree, for you, fruit without pips
I can spring-out of the stone for you, like water
I can paint your day-sky with my stars
I can do any magic, for you, without the wand

I can fly, I think ...

I can ...

I can, therefore I think ...

And thinking of you is like sitting next to the fireplace.
Only this fire has no one-place

Its everywhere.

Here

I stopped here,
on my way home.
I stopped
stopped here, as everyone must.

I lodged here

Here is where a seed was planted,
right here, next to the mill.

Here, here the river divides
and fish close their eyes when they sleep.

Here are the cradle, the flag and the torch,
here the sword was forged
and the scales of justice calibrated.

Here icons speak
and every discourse is a prayer,
every tree is a tree of life
and every plant a healing herb.

Here not everyone can come,
but from here all paths diverge.

Here dew never evaporates,
sunsets are fast and short and days are slow and long.
Here the sun has no time for romantics
and the moon is always full of wisdom.

Finally I woke up
here,
heard your voice
and listened, listened, listened
I couldn't recognise you.

Fisherman
(or how to recover memory from interpretation)

I think without an accent
but that's not how I talk.
I dream about water and swimming.
Awake, I find myself running through watermelon fields
miles of them
bumpy.
Reality is full of cracks -
that's how the light gets in
and that's how
I get to see it.
The light, not reality.

I want to walk back to the womb
Back to dreaminess, warmth
rhythm and rhyme.
But I end up just penetrating
back and forth, forth and back
thinking of swinging as being a journey
to somewhere.
Thinking not believing.
Talking not feeling.

I sit by the pond.
They call me a Fisherman;
there is no term for someone who is teaching fish about the
hook.
And when I am done with this swamp
I will move on to rivers
and oceans
and everywhere, everywhere

Mirror Mirror

when I first met her, her eyes
they were an advertisement for happiness

when I second met her, I asked:
"what is your lucky number"
"I can make any number happy"

and yes, before I third met her
my numbers came up, number after
number, first time, second time, every time

when I fourth met her, my eyes
were video cameras, recording
something to watch while eyes closed

and since I fifth met her
my eyelashes became lips,
that just kiss her, kiss her, kiss with every blink

before I sixth met her, I rang
her doorbell, and the song of that ring,
still rings, rings in my ring

later, at night – when I seventh met her –
I opened my eyes and it was dark
she opened her eyes and made a rainbow

when I lost-count-met-her
counting counted for nothing
my mirror-mirror stopped working

Insomnia in a Daydream

I plant a seed
every night
and start climbing a tree

I build a road, every night
one-way street
with a roundabout at its end

I build a beehive, every night
as if the dream was a honey
I build a beehive! but find it hard to be – every night, every
night

I build a house
brick by brick by brick
every night   every   night

what house takes more than a year to build?
365 days and 1 night. One night!
which tree takes more than a year to bear fruit?
365 days and 1 night! One night.

An uninvited guest, took a residence
and talks
talks to me in whisper, as if it wants to put me asleep
but
the snore-of-silence,
the noise-of-being-awake is deafening
I cannot not hear
I cannot not hear

Steps,
steps so strong
March,
so firm

leaves footsteps on my pillows
on my ceiling   on my walls
my bones   inside my skull

I dream to sleep.
one dream, same dream, one dream, same dream
same eyes   same, same   open eyes

one dream, one fruit
that one fruit on the top
of the tree, leafs of nightmares

words   words   Be my long hands
words   words   Be my wings

from one side of the mere to the other   across the ocean
of no sleep
there is a port of rest,
there is a port of madness
and I swim and I swim and I swim

Tense Free

I walk other people's dogs and look
out through someone else's window.
I start reading books from where
others leave bookmarks.
I look back and my gaze is
fixed on what is to come.
I reflect on the present and see us
as grammar teachers changing the past-imperfect

into a tense-free perfect future.

Lifetime Warranty

I was in the market, like we all are.
I was in the market
for a lie.

Asked a friend, he said:
"Best look online".
Asked an enemy, he said:
"I have one you can borrow."

Thanks friend, too many options.
Thanks enemy, but I want my own.

Passion for the impossible
led me to the department store – stories of it.
"Where is your lie-department", I asked?
"What kind of a lie would you like, sir?"

"One that will work, with low maintenance.
One that has few spare parts.
One that will protect me from my thoughts.
One that will last, as if it were the truth.
One with a warranty. One and only – my one"

"All our lies are your lies.
All our lies come with a lifetime warranty.
You just need to choose your packaging.
Would you like one from our beauty range,
or would you prefer to go for size?
We also stock social-justice lies and environmental lies."

"Look, I've tried them before,
but they could barely survive a day.
I want just ONE with a lifetime warranty."

"Yes Sir, all our lies have a lifetime warranty."
"What a bargain, let me choose my packaging then!"
"As the lifetime of any lie is up to 24 hours after opening,
you need to keep packing it and unpacking it, that's all."

What, why, how? I started to complain,
but it was like talking myself out of the deal.
And as I know the trick now
I took my lie home.
If it lasts two nights,
I'll marry it on Sunday.

Slam

Last night in my deepest sleep I heard a noise.
Not loud enough to wake me, just to bring me to your presence.

Aware of you I completely ignored the sound,
not that there was anything to say, or to hear.

And you said – did you hear that crash in the basement?

Why did I jump? Why did I go and check?
Not to protect my property, not to save anyone's life, not to
…

When I got back, you were not there. Not there.
No matter how hard I closed my eyes.

Kidnapped

And, once again, when all the stars hide behind the
horizon, and unite into one.
Paint the dark sky into grey, red and blue. Restore the
shapes of birds and the
clouds. I open my wings and, in one snatch, I kidnap the
morning. I cover you
with my shadow, and we fly. Filled with lightness, free,
frivolous. We fly, hand

in hand blindfolded by sunlight. We chat, we talk, we laugh,
we are quiet. And
you sing, we sing, to scare the night away. And I talk and
we talk, we speak the
same tongue, have same fears. We talk ourselves into
another day: friends, lovers, family. We play, we laugh, we
tell truth, we lie, we dream, we run, we promise,
we lust, we fly. Away from that scary night, away.

When sun crashes over the hard edge horizon and
breaks up into the many stars, again. The darkness
blinds me with special kind of silence,
one that bodes danger, muteness that
yells at me: "Talk, tell me: what were
you saying behind my back?". Clouds
fall heavy and I hear the whisper:
"Give me your hand, I am good for you,
I'll light the candles, entertain you, tell
jokes. I'll take off my clothes and sprinkle
my body with lightness, laughter, lust and
promise. Remember me? Spread your wings,
we can fly together. I howl my reply

as I try
to hide
in the shadows
of the birds.

Monday, the day after Sinday

Now that you know!
I have that smiley face again,
like I am not carrying a secret.
Now that I know, I silently celebrate the day I met you.

Light-hearted, I count up our meetings,
and I am so happy when I miss one
so I have all the more joy remembering it.

And I jump higher and higher like a frog,
striving to gain the same perspective of our love
that you have as you fly past.

If I could only get rid of this seventy-two-hour-erection;
as if I could stop thinking.

We are travelling on a straight road,
impatient for the next curve
so we can lean into each other.

We are celebrating now, before a fear of aging
replaces our fear of death.
Then, we will have to get to know
each other all over again.

And what is it, this Monday?
If it is not hunger, thirst, lust, fear, jealousy?

And does it matter what it is?
when there is so much love in you
so you can even love him
at one and the same time.

And that, that up till now I was always right
means nothing.Not even, that I ever was.

Man = Heart (From 5 to 5 till 5 past 5)

What does a man do when he wakes up at 5am
and you are at 3pm, so far away?

Man walks, and is happy
He is happy because the earth is round;
in whichever direction he goes,
man is closer to you.

Another dream, another 2+3=5
Us 2: you at 3pm, together at 5am.
Time is passing.
Man is counting the time with his heart.
So long as there is a heart there will be time.

I put batteries in the watches.
They function well –
the hands chase each other,
but they only mimic my heartbeat.
And it goes like this (sudden, unexpected chorus)
2 2 3, 2 2 3, 2 2 3, 2 2 3, 2 2 3
And it goes like that 5 times
And it goes like that until 5 to 5

What does a heart do when it wakes up at 5am?
What does it do when it wakes up at 5am
and you are at 3pm, so far away?

Heart walks, and is happy.
It is happy because my body is round.
In which ever direction it goes,
the heart Is closer to you.

It drums in my ears, waters my eyes
makes my cheeks flush, my jaw tremble.
Bites my Adam's apple,

tingles down my chest.
It scatters the butterflies in my stomach,
climbs the highest point
of the supine, round body.
Lingers there, for a looooong moment,
pulsating.

The heart spirals down the leg,
slides on a smooth part,
holds on to some of the hairs,
brushes the inside of the knee,
defines the muscles,
runs over the foot,
counting the toes
(silently in the background 2 2 3, 2 2 3).

It comes back in a hurry;
glides over hips, heals scars,
goes down the crack,
stays in the bush,
lingers there, for a loooooooong moment,
echoing, hanging on by the thread of your imagination.

And it goes like this (long-awaited chorus)
2 2 3, 2 2 3, 2 2 3, 2 2 3, 2 2 3
And it goes like that 5 times.
And it goes like that until 5 past 5.
Another day   Another dream
Another 2+3=5
And it goes like this ... one more time:
2 of us   3rd dimension   5th element
(2 2 3, 2 2 3 ... fades away)
So long as there is a heart,
there will be time
So long as there is a beat,
there will be rhythm.
Watches only measure the past.

Out of Step Parade

I build my house in the swamp,
I plant my garden in the desert,
foundations of foam, mesh walls, tinfoil roof.
    My body of wax, mind of dust.

In the evening I pour and re-pour water
from my room into the garden,
I count drops, wind, extinct stars;
all the sheep have drowned.
Instead of a rooster, frogs wake me up.
Not thinking about you – only dreaming of a dry morning.

In step with myself, out of step with you,
you illusory beings.
In step with you, out of step with myself,
you watery world.

If only I could go back to the Stone Age,
where there were no Stone cities or streets,
no dilemmas or fears cast in Stone,
    Only us and our Stone love.

If only I could go back to the Light Age,
where there were no dark cities or streets,
no dark dilemmas or fears,
endless days, you and me.
And night?
Only the shadow of our love.

We hold hands –
there is danger in every place we go, you said.
Let's take the side-roads, I said.
Keep in step.

Did you slow down? Did you speed up? Were you scared?
Was I hesitating? Did I start running?
Did I wait too long? Did I lose my way?

We fell out of step.

Now, I renounce you. I don't want you!
Neither as girlfriend, nor as wife.
Nor mother, sister, cousin or friend.

I don't want to know about you,
don't want to remember you,
don't want to know who or where you are.

If you could only be a baker so in the morning I could buy
bread from you; a taxi-driver, secretary, shop assistant,
blind accordion player. If you could only be a priest so I
could come every Sunday and confess; chef, waitress,
random passer-by. If you could only be a whore
so I could pay for a night with you.

Now
I build my house in the swamp,
I plant my garden in the desert,
Foundations of foam, mesh walls, tinfoil roof.
     My body of wax, mind of dust.

In the evening I pour and re-pour water
from my room into the garden,
I count drops, wind, extinct stars;
All the sheep have drowned.
Instead of a rooster, frogs wake me up.
Not thinking about you –
only dreaming of a dry morning.

In step with myself, out of step with you,
you illusory beings.
In step with you, out of step with myself,
you watery world.

I was close, so close to that one final Labyrinth.

six days and one Wednesday

One,
Trust tattooed on a heart, ridges of unity
carved into the brain.
Two magnets melded into stainless steel,
A melody composed with two notes,
Poetry written with two words,
A rainbow of two colours,
Reality made from two dreams.

One creates the sense of its existence. To be.
Let us be!   To skin
you give the sense of touch.
And I will taste for you.   To the face
you give your smile,
and me, I will be two ears,
at the corners of your smile.   To our kiss
you give the sense of taste.   To eyes
you create the sense of sight.
You be an eye. And I will be an eyelid.

So while we sleep I can cover you
And when we are awake
I caress you
     with every blink.
You be me   I give you life.
I be you   given life.

That done, let's create the sense of flying
With angel's wings for us to fly high
so we can fathom our depths.
And then to Cupid people in love,
Your right, my left. Your arrow, my bow.

Then create the sense of dreaming
To dream pure dreams, divine dreams – like humans do,

In pre-language, with pre-colours. In pre-dimensions.
Dreams as yet unwritten in the history of dreams.
And simple dreams, human dreams –like gods do,
dream about One, about something that we already are.

To dream about other people's weddings and separations
You, my dream
      I, reality of your dream.
And in the morning, you be our patience,
And I will be our strength.
One patience. One strength. One dream.

We can build the sense of endlessness
And run, run through sleepy meadows,
To sow happiness.
Run through vineyards in bloom,
Into the arms of the vintage,

Into the arms of the harvest of happiness,
To stamp on the grapes
Your left, my right. Wine for us, happiness for One.

Create the sense of wandering
And endlessly wander through our treasure map,
in slippers of promises let's stumble around through love's labyrinth.

And create One's sense of forgetfulness
So we can forget we once rode on a donkey of separation
into the stable of waiting.
Forget Waiting
and the memory of waiting and the possibility of waiting.
Forget Bared teeth of love and red scratch marks of disbelief;
Traffic lights of disagreement on an intersection;
And all the other overplayed love scripts
Forget the feeling of forgetting.
Forget the memory of the feeling of forgetting.

We chisel on a gravestone for dead love,
chisel and chisel until it turns into dust…
…and the wind spreads that dust like ashes,
and rain washes those ashes down onto the earth,
and the earth feeds that dust to orchards of new beginnings,
pre-sin love Edens.

And …one more thing … Let us have one truth, one lie,
And only one secret,
Ours.
Have one peace and one lust, And one sin … only one,
Ours.

You be light, I'll be shadow, Me, your only thought and you the only meaning of that thought.

Unity: Magnetic light, ray of gravity, moonlit days,
Glass metal, mirror of passion, diamond of life.
One.
I heart, you soul. I in-breath, you out-breath.
Up and down. Water and fire.
Serenity and lust. Wave and rock.
Love and indifference. Life and death.
One.

Let's create the sense of universe,
To watch the half-moon from the earth
And to have a star where we can watch this half-world
And to find a planet with many moons,
Just for the romantics.

And if we ever, ever separate
You keep all the senses for yourself.
For me leave only One,
The sense of memory.

Spinning the Real

It was raining and one young girl, my mother to be, rushed into the cinema for shelter. There was nobody at the box office. So she walked into the dark but predictable theatre and found a seat. After the movie she realised it was still raining outside. She liked that movie, it was so real, so she stayed for another session. It's been raining for 9 months now.

The young man who wasn't at the box office was my father to be. He had been popping corn since he was 14. At 16 he was an expert; they even allowed him to sell tickets. And ice cream. Now he is spinning the reel.

When I was born in Japan, it was not November. Nor it was the month when cherry blossoms. I really wanted to be born an Aries. Not just because I was a sheep in a previous life. So I waited patiently. Waited waited … for the rain to stop. For the corn to pop. For an I to scream.

When the day came it was just like a movie premiere. Big noise, press-push, red sheets, bright lights. It was May, or it might have been June. The month that most great movie directors were born in. Like that big, fat one that made those scary cult movies. Or that guy with glasses that filmed the best comedies. I grew to like the young long-haired one even after he had a bad haircut.

And I popped the corn, I creamed the ice and I sold tickets. Spinning the real.

Striptease

invited back into your memory
like many times in the past, unlike any time before

remembering, involves time-travel;
I take my time and I put on
my old clothes so you recognise me

memory
is taking time, is dressing up
and putting make-up
on things that may have happened,

on arrival –
charisma of memory leaves us speechless
and more scared than any future could have done

we strip ... no need for words, words anyway...
are just clothes worn by our thoughts,

naked ... thoughts traverse
like two flies having sex mid-air
memory is re-memorised

we strip... thoughts are only clothes worn by our feelings.
and feelings? feelings are clothes
worn by our instincts

naked ... again ... and again
you naked, striped naked
so totally naked - reduced to a smell,
of a future,
of a home still not built,
of a newborn who is trying to remember its name.

Time Speaks

Its seconds and minutes create
the symphony of hours and days;
a dictionary of ticks and tacks;
a thesaurus of tricks and tracks;
glossary of waiting and avoiding;
a song of yesteryear and posterity.
A song that is most unlistenable, un-understandable
unless you daydream.

In a daydream, we can talk about time
but we think space.
Make time! Make space!
For lotus flowers to pop up in the muddy sky
and its petals make steps,
choreograph our dance.

Sometimes sky is blue,
like a lake with big white swans.
Swan necks are touching the earth
so we can climb and swim
in the lake.
Dance on lotus petals
dance   dance
on the fluffy white swans.

Summer Love

Yes, yes! that's it –
keep still for me, please; let me just look at you.

You are so gorgeous, inflated like that,
you are so shiny and round, wet and pumped up.

Let's go and play in the fountain –
that way u can not run too far away from me.

No, I am not going to jump on you.
I know you don't like sand.
Ok, ok, I will take you on the grass.

No! I am not barking, I am just thinking aloud.
I am saying how much I like you.

Yes, of course I love you.
I wish for a leash, but you say you are
not sure how strong is my commitment.

Please, bounce for me a little.
It's so awesome running around and feeling you
rubbing your rubber against my fur.

No, no. I didn't say relationship.
I just said you look like most magnificent ship
when u jump in the water.

Chasing you is making my thoughts so vague.
Open your air plug a little –
my tail is erect and wagging.

No, I don't want you to change.
I like you just the way you are:
aerated, exorbitant, Sky-high.

Ok ok ok don't run away. I am going
to calm down. No I'm not hugging trees.
I'm just de-sharpening my claws not to hurt you.

let's do it now, let's do it on the beach
let's do it doggy style!

I sit, I roll over, I give a paw
no I don't want a cookie. I want you, you, you!

you, you, you and not any other beach ball
Don't say its impossible. On the way home we will
cuddle up in the booth and everything is going to be
possible.

No matter how hard this puppy will find the way to
pick you up before winter
when deflated beach balls go into the storage
and puppies fall in love
with used tennis balls.

Superhero

He holds his breath
in front of the mirror.
Angst. Taciturn. Seditious.
As if he is just about to be arrested,
for impersonating himself.
In his spare room.
In his spare life.

His story has been long written;
he has only to perform now –
something that feels like an ending.
Perfunctory. Lingering. Theatrical.
In one move
one narrowing horizon.

Vast personality confined into a single character.
Desultory. Otiose. Featureless.
A superhero reduced to his cape.

The Golden Boat

I had this ticket for the long long time
And when I came to the boat they said it's not my time yet
How did they know? I wanted to ask
I didn't even show them the ticket
they didn't show me the time

And the sails went up
The boat left, leaving me drifting
Golden Boat
too big for my eye, too small for my foot.

The Golden Boat with silvery-white sails
like a ghost.

I started yelling. Waving messages
Ghost to ghost.

Sometimes listening to echoes can be a conversation
Sometimes shouting into echo can be calling yourself
Sometimes hearing an echo can be heard as a call

and jump into the sea
Forgetting that I don't know how to swim
I started hugging water as if I could hold on to it
As if something that you are drowning into
can save you from drowning.

To make someone who doesn't want to hear you,
hear you.
Is as easy as biting your own ears.

Why they didn't want to see my ticket?
How did they know?
I'll ask.
Once I reach the boat

The Heart Asks for Pleasure First

Morning, delivered by raindrops;
ocean winds stacked with greyness.
Kind of greyness that makes your
heart and soul into a grey matter.
So you can think and smell.

I can not find my windows –
they are the same colour as the walls.
As if we were thrown up
to the heavy clouds for breakfast.

Our earth, centre of the universe,
looks like it's beaming with light.

The trees are reaching out
bare branches to welcome us back.

I can understand by smelling:
Spring means promise in every language.
But this New Zealand Spring smells
more like sacrifice.

Reminds me of Michael Nyman's
score for the movie Piano:
sharply soft and lightly heavy,
strikes every chord, cuts every cord.
Can make every baby go to sleep
and every man or women cry.
I could never tell the difference
between tracks: Promise and Sacrifice.

The Nine Circles of Heaven

This path I travelled today from sky to sky
Through the nine circles of heaven.

Wandering through your deepest thoughts
I found a shortcut to your dreams.
Plunging into your essence
I planted my standard on your hill.

Breaking the barrier
between tenderness and pain,
I bridged the river of your innocence
but drowned in the sea of your lust.

I follow you,
as you stroll down mysterious paths.
I smooth your curves
and sheath your softness.
I inhale your whisper,
my every sigh counting your breath.
I walk into my shadow
and step through mirrors.
My eyes lead your way,
light so you can carry me,
bright so you can see me,
free from care so you can trust me.

With every move
I leave a trail of raging desire.
I listen to you, telling me something half-asleep.
Something beautiful.
Something as yet unwritten
in the history of beautiful dreams.

Before I fall asleep I catch myself
Telling lullabies to our grandchildren.

Visionary Indecisiveness

I look at my arts and parts, at my articles and particles.
I look at my green and my lime, at my sentence and my time.
I look at my tensions and dimensions, at the whole and the holes.

Why am I this mile-wide highway
from here to there?
How long must I be this multi-coloured scarecrow
on an Arctic field of snow?
What use is there being a lone raindrop
at the bottom of the ocean?
Who would choose to be a nuclear-powered ice-breaker
in the middle of the desert?

I ask me   for no answer
    I challenge me   without a demand
        I approve of me   by proving myself wrong.

I leave my garden of imagination open
to others for planting
as I rejoice in this state of homeless domesticity.

Thoughts flow down sunny slopes,
emotions roar like a winter waterfall.
My heart is the size of a spoonful of food
offered to Africa;
ideas unfurl like fern leaves.
Fears ebb and flow like inner-sea tides,
my love a tsunami in waiting.

Awareness is just the narrow pipeline of the present.
I keep expanding that perspective,
but the pipe can never take the extra volume.

The Place where Something-Outside-of-You is Thinking

I stand
overcast
by the quiet lake
trying to distinguish
between green and grey
between pale green and pale gray
                between pale and pale

sky reflected in the lake   lake reflected in the sky
thoughts, clouds, leaves, fish and rocks

floating weightlessly somewhere
in the gradient overlay

internally uninterruptible, saturated with stillness
                            horizonless bliss
      perfect and dry, homogenous and majestic
              like a two-dimensional crystal

*

salience conquered by silence
significance by essence
meaning by sense
*

a sort of a fizz appears on the left
and bubbles spread, in an instant
... bubbles ...
as if lake's cells are dividing
maybe it's a feeding time for the fish, or shells at the bottom
are opening
air driven out by the wind of tide
... ripples ...

that must look like fireworks to fish and shells
... ripples ...
that soundly bump into other ripples
making infinite number of eternity symbols
 like kisses
triangulate and unite again in euphonic symmetry
as if two invisible thousand-legged spiders are dancing
dancing on the surface
on the surface

it takes a while for my imbued skin to tell me
its raining

Pure Noise

open one song in two windows
and play them one minute apart
space can be divided; soundcannot
time can be spent; spacecannot

we are all tinder
this song may be
a burned butterfly

as engaging as listening
to an argument
in a foreign language
for far too long

space in the middle of time
windows between sounds
time between silences

There, Maybe

I confess
I became a courageous coward,
a bee on wheels without a sting,
a bear who drinks artificial pears,
an angel with a tail.

I confess
There's something I want to add,
- not that my words will mean anything to anyone -
it is easy to confess guilt.
How do I confess innocence?
when I am punished already
by your absence.

For three days you sent me flowers,
without even knowing my name.
You painted my dreams,
taught my heart to beat a new rhythm.
You uncovered my smile, awoke my gentleness,
fed my lust, kept me in Springtime.

I start everything in the middle
and finish before the end,
knowing it will pass, knowing it can never be.
Still I lose myself in the bliss of this moment.

Consciously you left, unconsciously you left traces.
I return, I recognise the non-hidden…

Confess!
You are running away
towards a freedom behind bars,
Shaking the bars –
your phantom of freedom
continues to travel his path of light

at the speed of a snail,
leaving a glow in your eyes.

How long did it take me to learn to speak?
In an instant I have to learn
to be silent.

How long did it take you to learn to speak?
In an instant you have to learn
to be silent.

And when we get There, where light doesn't refract,
where night is day ,east is west, winter is summer;
where freedom is the same as security
where the present is as good as the past
where the Cross and the Crescent,
the star of David are one.

There maybe, I will find a way to say
I love you.

Part III: Poems about Us

Sixty Nine

let's fire the candles
let's talk a little talk
drink a little drink
look at each other, look at the stars
let's listen to ocean waves made by the bouncing moon

and then orbit the earth for 7 days in permanent sunset
till hot wax shapes replace clouds
and divine pre-Eden fruits cover the mountains
and glorious-ivory-ocean-flames overshadow the darkness
of unknown

if u still remember me

www.ingramcontent.com/pod-product-compliance
Lightning Source LLC
Chambersburg PA
CBHW070649300426
44111CB00013B/2342